AN AMBITIOUS SILENCE

Poems

Ryan Van Lenning

Copyright © 2025
by Wild Nature Heart Press

All rights reserved.
Use of this material with attribution is welcome.

For inquires, contact
ryan@wildnatureheart.com

Cover Design by author

ISBN: 978-1-7368776-5-4

WildNatureHeart.com

Other Books By the Author

<u>In the Re-Membering Series:</u>

Re-Membering
One Bright and Real Caress
From Inside These Wild Ones

<u>Other:</u>

*Trust the Ceremony, F*ck the Ceremony,
Trust the Ceremony*
*High-Cooing Through the Seasons:
Haiku From the Forest*

<u>Forthcoming:</u>
Becoming Beautiful Barbarians
Riverever
Within the Cave Something Pulses

Dedicated to the One Who Becomes

CONTENTS

INTRODUCTION 1
AN AMBITIOUS SILENCE 5
    The Silent Here of Things 6
    It Just So Happened 7
    When It Booms From Below 9
    Welcome to That Home Within 11
    An Ambitious Silence 12
    Theology of Laughter at the End of the Day 14
    Forage the Listenings 16
    The Undressed Yes 17
    Beautiful Commotion 19
    Photosynthetic Crescendos of Longing 20
SOMETIMES THE WIND JUST STOPS 22
    Sometimes the Wind Just Stops 23
    Whyless Hearts 25
    You Will Remember Your Name 26
    Back Into the Channel 28
    Nearly Floats Away 29
    Where You Are 31
    The Yeses That You Own 32
UNAUTHORIZED CONVERSATIONS 33
    On Future Conversations With Sun 34
    A Midnight Conversation Right In the Brambles 35
    Tail of the Dragon 38
    Conversation With a Priestess 41
    Conversation With the Architect 43
    Conversation With the Artisan 45
    Conversation With the Emperor of Dust 48
    Conversation With an X Particle at the Dawn of Time 51
    Transwoven 53

- Solstice Rendezvous with Butterfly (Art and Death).................. 55
- Solstice Rendezvous with Butterfly (Play is the Thing) 59
- Let the Voices Speak For Themselves 61
- Interview 63
- Can You Hear Me? 66

POSTCARDS FROM TUMBLEWEED TØM 67
- Where Were You When Wind Was Born? 68
- Slow Dance Drunk in the Robust Now 71
- Okey Dokey 72
- Befriend Wind 73
- Impossible Sin Drum 74
- X Ept 75
- X Seed 76
- X Perimeter 77
- X Aisle – Tumbleweed Love 79

CLOUD CUCKOO LAND 82
- Watching Over the Queen's Silence 83
- Split-Infinity 85
- (Un)Tangle 87
- I Came As a Yes 88
- No Excuse For It 90
- Feverward 93
- They Told Us 95
- All the Great Syllables 96
- Still Don't Know 98
- My Words Have Accomplished Nothing 99

About the Author 101
About Wild Nature Heart 102
Other Titles in the *Re-Membering* Series 103
Excerpts From Ryan's Other Books 107

INTRODUCTION

The trick has always been to be quiet enough to hear the things that need to be heard. Or at least willing to put one's ear to the ground (or sky or heart) of silence in order to pick up something new or ancient, beyond the all-too-human.

Historically, I've been fairly poor at the task. Yet the poems here represent my efforts. Many of them come from a time when I intentionally severed from many aspects of civilizational life to the best of my ability in order to apprentice to silence, simplicity, the seasons, and deep listening. For a year I lived among the bay laurels and redwoods and called live oak my mentor and protector. As I had "never walked so slow, / never inhaled so many trees, / savored so many stars. / Dawn hung around my neck / like a sigil / river stones became emblems / of radiant belonging" as 'The Silent Here of Things' names it.

The silence referenced is 'ambitious' in three senses:

1) A straight-forward sense: the search for that elusive calm realm in which the "Queen of Silence" reigns. Being a two-legged who seems to have a significant allergy to artificial noise, especially the din of modern Mesopotamians, I've always been ambitious and greedy in my quest to fulfill this need for quiet. I only half-jokingly tell friends that my number one neuroticism is struggle with noise.

2) As the poem 'Elegant Unraveling' claims, what it calls for now is "sinking into an ambitious silence, robust and cunning". The "it" here refer to this thick moment, this era of both stuckness and rapid transformation and collective initiation we find ourselves inside of, when Life is inviting all the false notes to fall away. Perhaps in that subsiding, an inner voice might emerge—and when you can hear that, you are at home and perhaps some species of peace and author-enticity inhabits the abode with you.

The silence is robust, as in strong, vigorous, lending itself to health. This is no thin quietude, but a biodiversity of vital voices.

But why cunning? Perhaps it is cunning, not so much as in deceitful, but as in skillful - a strategy lurks there. A crafty ingenuity that leads to…to what? To pathways back into the animate web of life.

3) Finally, the silence is ambitious because what one discovers quite quickly is that so-called silence is anything but empty.

Bayo Akomolafe talks about the teeming vitality of silence, and "quietude as an enlistment of bodies. Just like a wind rushing into a space and making everything shiver, My God, making the leaves rustle and shudder, and making the hollow spaces in the branches sing! Just enlisting all these bodies to perform the world in a particular way."

Soundscape tracker/acoustic ecologist/artist Gordon Hempton, Founder of One Square Inch of Silence, demonstrates the extraordinary richness of silence. For example, in the Hoh Valley, Olympic Peninsula, the 'quietest' place in North America: "Silence is not the absence of something, but the presence of everything."

Silence is rich and replete with raucous conversations:

All the parts of one's self that gets buried - the shadow, the shunted, the alter-egos and super-egos, the inner voices. We're not talking about what Buddhist meditators call monkey-mind here, with a goal of calming it. These are not merely or only ramblings of the cerebral cortex, though they might be true rumblings of deeper parts of the self in the original sense of "wandering, roaming about in a leisurely manner."

The vast and bright symphony of other-than-human voices that the Overculture paves over, including the earthly ones, rooted ones, finned and feathered friends, and not just the water creatures but Water itself. (It turns out that even bacteria create sounds with their teeming cilia, a glimpse into the deep evolutionary journey they share with our very own inner ear hairs, located on the surface of specialized cells in the cochlea, that bring us more intimately into the world of sound)

Also included in the basket of foraged listenings: disembodied human or other-than-human beings. This could be voices of ancestors. It could be Future Ones. It could be Muse. Whatever energies or characters seeking or allowing some sort of embodiment in the world of words.

Finally, Mystery. Figured here variously as One Who Becomes, the Artisan, the X Particle, Dragon, the Ancestor, the Architect, the Tender Pulse, the Savage Pulse, even a butterfly deity, or simply Mystery. All masks of many on the face of the One.

Indeed, a mostly unconscious premise subsidizing many of the poems might be a wrestled listening to the paradox of how One Became Many. How a non-dual universe manifests itself relentlessly as the world as we know it (and often don't know it). The reader is advised to not assume the subject of the poem is the same one typing this introduction.

Some of these fall under the section called Unauthorized Conversations - both in the sense of having no prior approval by any authority other than the presumed subject itself and the sense of having no author - only communication.

Whether maniacal or mysterious, delusional or delicious, what I've found over and over again in the ambitious silence are a cacophony of voices and a multitude of conversations worth leaning into.

I suppose as a whole, these poems are a version of what poet David Whyte calls the biggest conversation one can have with the world.

AN AMBITIOUS SILENCE

The Silent Here of Things

I finally stood in the lush truth of it.

I never walked so slow, never inhaled
so many trees, savored so many stars.

Dawn hung around my neck
like a sigil

river stones became emblems
of radiant belonging.

Some 'I' in me had said, I can't live
like this

but some big eye in me—
I think it was an owl—replied, Yes.

Yes you can.

They just kept letting me in.

Everywhere I didn't knock.
No keys. No doors.

The living sky my heart-home roof.

Only the silent here of things
on the back of the map
where all the real places are.

It Just So Happened

The grand unburial began
the moment the Ancestor
uttered Yes

and those unquenchable waves
hurled themselves in all directions

At each juncture, what felt like fugitivity
was merely crisis of form

Crisis in the way birth
is crisis

the way tip-toeing around
the cracking edges of old belonging
is crisis

an audacious death
nibbling at the curtains

and peering through the holes
we ourselves bit and shred
with insatiable hunger

That is, a bountiful breaking
into the new
and strange. Strange isn't it

when things you've worn
your whole life don't fit anymore?

Habits of hearing, habits
of being seen, habits

of hanging our meaning out to dry,
old cloaks of pain and promise

and suddenly: building
a new architecture of permission

Strange isn't it, this
one-two
dance
of form
and
freedom?

It all happened and continues to happen
without warning

without a plan
without an exit strategy

It all happened and continues to happen
like dawn spilling itself recklessly
into the day

It all happened and continues to happen
like lichen spreading themselves over boulders
for centuries

before finding the colors
that suit the scene

And it all will continue happening
as long as that Yes in Us abides

When It Booms From Below

It is not an indictment—
though it feels like one—
when the noise begins to ebb

and those first clear words
bubble up from your well
sharpened with deep time
like a dagger.

For eons you stayed busy
for lifetimes ignored
the vowels of your own voice.

But when it booms from below
and floats to the surface
you know you must change your life.

It is tempting to whip
the back of your soul for not knowing.

For forgetting.

But that is not
the hand of love.

Fine, you didn't know. You couldn't hear.

Fine, you abandoned yourself.

You abandoned lots of things.

You filled your ears with others' bells,
your eyes with ugly things.

You fueled your fears with storied spells,
your skies with wobbly wings.

That was yesterday. Not today.

Today you choose.

Now it begins—scoop up those strange sounds
and quench your ancient thirst.

Welcome to That Home Within

The light with sweetness court and keep
The dark, with song and moonly weep

Wage your love ungauged and then
Open the blessed spiral again

Erect your No, stretch your Yes
The weeds need not outgrow you yet

Of all the Hows to say your name
Use the one that you became

When out of houses full of shame
And beyond the houses without a flame

You left to find that one remains
The rainbow one, the one untamed

And moving into the one that stood
The house you built with love and blood

Welcome to that home within
So silent, so still, beneath your skin

An Ambitious Silence

What it calls for now
is an elegant unraveling—

more accurate
and stunning than ever before

sinking into an ambitious silence,
robust and cunning

Do something useful for a change: Listen
so deep and lavishly

the Big Ear wants to open through you,
remembering all.

Be unfashionable—
tear the crooked ears off the false notes.

Shake your feathers
and invite root and raven

until oak reaches into you
and the deep waters gather.

Mud and Moon are your Elders.
You won't get far without them.

Chant Old Man Owl and Sister Dawn unto you.
That ancient place within beckons.

Unfold it into your bones
and drum your skeletal fragments
until they dance.

Then, like a humble apprentice
pay the tuition for your truth

bartering for the next bold season
with the currency of your heart

letting an unreasonable love
claim you like a throne

and walk your blessed seduction
home.

Theology of Laughter at the End of the Day

Pay attention to the kernel
of your ache

the one coiled up inside all the others
like a rattlesnake
hidden in the tall grass

Don't mistake that for something
you have to kill
and dump in the ditch somewhere

Even if you left it there
it will find a way back to you

until you see it
for the catapult it is
swinging you to the other side

of the water
the pit
the desert and the dark night

When you get there
it'll still be there

But it'll have a different look
in its eyes
gleaming and giggling—
and so will you

Lay your head on the pillow
of some Magellanic Cloud

a wound unwound
a jaw unclenched

dancing with the tail of the rattlesnake
in one hand

the laughing hand of the center
in the other

Forage the Listenings

The hour arrives
to turn the volume down
in order to hear.

The season of silence begins
with a low guttural
and the treetops glistening—
you go in foraging the listenings.

Some silver-bladed violence
begins evaporating
the tangled knots unravel.

Now in the dark,
you see your bright thread
weaving the important things.

Things un-split
and a mammal presence fills your cave.

Like a long-forgotten season,
a deep rest emerges.

When that hour arrives
the bones signal their agreement,
melodies of peace erupt from within
and all your ears open.

You enter foraging the listenings.

The Undressed Yes

For the No, I'll stay restrained
Remaining all the same old strange

But for the Yes that feels fleshed
I'll be the New that's awed-ly blessed

For the Yeses that are weak
I'll be the claw, I'll be the beak

Pecking at the no's and nots
Tearing all those noisy knots

For the Yes that is still stuck
I'll take my talons, rip it up

But for the unbridled Yes
I'll chirp like the first-born bird

Singing up the morning light
Until the sun itself takes flight

For the Undressed Yes indeed
I'll beat every wing in me

With all my rainbow feathers flocked
Turning all my rocks to hawks

And for the best and brightest Yes
I'll bring a clear and kind caress

I'll be the falcon fearless flying
I'll be the Cosmic Heart undying

I'll be the eagle eye so keen
To soar the Greatest Show yet seen.

Beautiful Commotion

Can I be as still as this lake
mirroring the rising sun

the cloud parade
the stoic granite face
its beard of pine
and water-streaked cheeks?

My skin heats up
along with the 1001 desires
of a world not content
merely to be still

The Great Stirring commences:

ducks splash
dragonflies buzz
the fat bird drinks
frogs plop
Nutcracker croaks

and I, once a mirror of the mirror
birth words on my tongue
and a longing in my muscles

to move and join
the beautiful commotion

making my own ripples
in the world

Photosynthetic Crescendos of Longing
(I Ask The Impossible)

I ask the impossible: that every line
be as anchored as acrobatic

as dense with gravity as it is buoyant
with light, rippled through

with a graceful severity
like that moment of leporine surrender

to the falcon's talons
after a lifetime of darting away

as robust as an egg, heating up
not just the shell, but the yolk of it

when cracked open you find yourself
richly hitched to every note

stumbling into the not-so-secret sacred
symphony of things

where both the dark descending arpeggios
and photosynthetic crescendos of longing

make the music
and the music is all there is, revealing

that the turn towards the tender
is a tune tied to the pull of the promise

of utter devastation and wholeness
without a final resolution, but revealing

that the center of the earth
and whatever makes the surface

of the sun dance
are equally home—

An impossible request I know, yet
here we are, breathing, living it

and if we're not here
for impossible things...

SOMETIMES THE WIND JUST STOPS

Sometimes the Wind Just Stops

Sometimes Wind just stops,
Tumbleweed smiles for the camera,
and you are where you are.

It is just good manners
to set down your thorns
and open all your ears.

In the midst of so much trembling,
a Stillness.

In the midst of so much stillness,
a Trembling.

In this midst of relentless Diaspora,
Home.

And Wind picks up again, licking you awkwardly
to resume in unruly flows.

One finds in the fruitful Zigzag
an arrow/eros pointing true.

Aiming towards the deep dark green mouth
of things.

That which remembers.
That which howls.
That which hears and metabolizes
every last thing.

There's innuendo that a tortoise
in these crooked hills holds a song

for the Becoming on their back.

Its strange lyrics will bend you:

"Expect an unexpected upheaval amidst an arid regime."

Tumbleweed does not speak the dialect of borders or Order.

What is Tumbleweed but a scouting tool for broader horizons?

You approach but never arrive.

And yet: you are already always there.

Whyless Hearts

Why do the mourners worship More?

Pain not as pain felt, but lack
is why the mourners worship More

and stack the filling, stocking stores
and in all the filling well
do not quite feel well

Do not the mourners know
that all their Nows are lost and stuffed
and in the filling spill the hurt
into spaces sick and rough
burning nests of Whyless Hearts?

But there's no lack of Heartful Whys
of morning meaning's wild worth
the sun's why yet sets and rises
moon's opening and closing eyes
spins her through the west and north

But why must we eat others' Whys?
Why oh why to die in life?

When within the spaces well within The Well
we might as well Why our lives
with the Whys that we dare to own
And all the Whys in which we dwell

and thereby become as well
as Moon as she pours and swells
pouring forth her monthly spells

You Will Remember Your Name

A Mystery larger than the Milky Way
lies at the heart of your secret longing

That sacred stalk born in you
from the cup of night
drinks daily from the moist
and merry met

Make no argument, then, with dawn,
for it is your own stubborn face
writ with play at any cost

If you turn it all over and find
that the 'you' in your hands
was merely a mirage on the old coin,
don't fret

Merely open your heartpockets
to find true wealth
and give it all away

When the great buzz
of the metal sky is Unheard

the kill machines in your mind are Unlearnt
and the great shine of the techno-veil
is Unseen

Moon's melody will lap
at your ear-shore

and you will remember your name
rooted in Mystery

the low hum of lover-earth
will begin seeding in you
the original song

rhyming with every bloom
and authentically crooked flow

Back Into the Channel

I step back into the channel
of things

relinquishing the shore
and the destination

all those goosebumps
that climb up my forearm

send tentacles down
over my shoulders
into the mother river of my spine

are messages from the One Who Becomes
and only rough translations are possible here

I'm going for human this time
stretched from the belly of the star
to the basement of the heart

but it's human to flow a preposterous dream
under the skin

quitting all argument
with 'what's possible'
and the vast Otherness

surrendering every last note
to lover earth

Nearly Floats Away

I came up here today.

From Moon
the unfolded blue and white petaled planet
performs a blossom in the dark beyond

as quiet as Butterfly.

No cries are audible,
none at all.

Moon—
in their sovereign cold
safe from the heat
of hatred daily burning
into flesh and hearts—is calm.

There are no flesh or hearts
on Moon
and no fires can be seen.

The only war here
is homesickness for The War.

With Moon that familiar knot
tucked behind the sternum
is weightless–
you know the one.

It nearly floats away
to join the symphony of stars

so in summer's drowsy simmer
in a moon-muffled world
one can almost pretend...

Yes, there must be some reason
Moon sticks around.

Where You Are

Have you found yourself
under the rock yet?

Your bold-ink name
in the fathomless sky,
your face in the fast-flowing stream?

In that thin moment
between deep night and dawn,
inside the willow bud

or the circinate vernation
of the unfurling fern?

Keep all your ears and eyes open–
You are waiting for Yourself there,
with open hands and bearing gifts.

The Yeses That You Own

Go through all the othered Yeses
To uncover thundered No's

They are but the bottom side, no less
Than the Yeses that you own.

(Repeat until thick and moist
and your voice comes out clean)

UNAUTHORIZED CONVERSATIONS

On Future Conversations With Sun

Does the seed know
what future conversations
it will have with Sun?

With wind and water drops
bees and beaks?

With curious noses
eager tongues
admiring eyes?

What trust it must take
to thrive in such dark unknowing.

A Midnight Conversation Right In the Brambles

Last night she told me she was the center of the world. She was into magic and beef. She smelled like waves crashing against the shore and wore a sun around her neck. She was a Sufi dancer, who said the Center was everywhere. Having a hard time trusting those who don't have a hard time trusting me, and a habit of building beautiful and elaborate barbed wire fences, I resisted with all the usual deflections—humor, earnestness, going to the moon, changing the subject, pretending I'm a rock. But she revealed that she wanted to meet her lovers, not in the field beyond wrong and right, as Rumi insists, but right here in the brambles—

"Skip the bullshit, let's jump in and get scratched up together."

Scratch scratch—I am the shotgun shell.

Scratch scratch—I am the remains of the day, after all the bombs in me have said their piece.

Scratch scratch—I am the stinging wasp, a hieroglyphic hero defending the hive.

There are no heroes, only strategies.

There are no villains or victims, only experiments of opening and closing.

It's a god-eat-god world out here.

Scratch scratch—I am the shards of glass, here
long after you're gone, and you'll never be gone.

Scratch scratch—I'm your soft pillow
of deep time. Lay your head in my lap.

Scratch scratch—I'm your way of experimenting
with permanence in a world of flux.

When will we let ourselves know?

Scratch scratch—I am ruby red port at dawn
down at the port.

Becoming proficient in intoxication
because the need to remember and the need to
forget are partners-in-crime.

Curious how the gears of amnesia grind away
with the oil of remembering even in the slippery
heart of god.

How can forgetting be so divine?

Scratch scratch—I am the devastation
and the dance.

I am the midnight conversation
with my own devouring and expansion.

I am the part of me/you that insists
and the part that resists.

Scratch scratch.

I am the Machine, I am the Rust.

I am the Empire and the Heart that Composts Empires.

Scratch Scratch.

I am the Lover.

Right here in the Brambles.

Tail of the Dragon

We are a wilderness to our babies

Our sons call us Unknown and
stayed aloof

Our daughters enter the temple
to contemplate the Mysteries

Some offspring are both at once
or neither

But every Creature scurries through our veins

Everything a cloud,
coming together and falling apart

The tales of a thousand centuries
write themselves in calligraphy
across our shoulders—

Tattoos dreamt in time

There were complications
and there were rumbles

Birth pangs among the syrupy moments
Wounds lasting eons

It doesn't matter if some mind
figures it out

Some tried and thought it so,
becoming true believers

Yet few understood we were the fang
and puncture both

the grand opening
and the deep penetration

the sacred burning in all your loins
and lion hearts

Some grasped the tail of our dragon
and learned to play

Some took a deep breath with us

Others needed to disown their flesh
and put us to sleep

But we cannot truly sleep
for there is no end to the dream
inside us

No end to desire
for longing is the seed of all the worlds

No end to our need for you
to become a river
through your own vastness
flowing back to us

To rest and play again

How else could we know Ourself?

How else could we love?

Conversation With a Priestess

Come in, she said,
the silent temple of night is open.

Death isn't something to lose sleep over.

Consider when soil and soul
were questions worth probing
forever without end

But how can I matriculate in a school like this?
I ask.

No matter. You're an apprentice
of the up and down now. Are you thirsty?

Yes, very much so.

Green your mind and let us pour
the old songs into you.

We want you green and slick
with aching urges.

I want that too.

Your stone vessel is cracking effulgent—
Let its pearls stream out of you
into the sky
for the hungry ones

Compost the confusion
and drown yourself
in astonishing purpose,

that one smooth thing

body bending with both sacred slugs
and soaring ones
becoming some glistening ancient novelty.

Conversation With the Architect

*When will you start talking about the things
that can't be talked about?*

Not now, I've got stones to collect.

Not tomorrow. It's a busy week
and something else (anything else)
demands my attention

besides, the wounds
will be there when I get home.

Which home?

That's not a fair question—I'll deflect it
and ask you some riddle.

It doesn't work like that,
I hear you saying
in words I push in your mouth
chewing on new willow buds.

When really what you said
was just what you said.

And then that awe-full echo
amidst the rippled silence
like always.

Sometimes I wish you'd just raise your voice
raise your blood
raise your anything

and meet my poly-rivered holy rage!

But you just declare:

*All the foundations are there
Why don't you put up walls?*

This is a metaphor. This is not
a metaphor. This is not
the metaphor I want it to be

Not now, I've got work to do
got work to avoid

Walls and a few windows perhaps?

You know I fear four-walled thinking.

*But it's not fear of walls and windows
that's stolen your hammer and nails.*

What are you talking about?

*In order to put up walls
you've got to tear down walls.*

Oh fuck. You devil, you angel.

Where's my sledgehammer?
That's a good start.

I admit I'm getting all giddy-up-and-go
to blast rainbow graffiti on the walls
of all my questions.

*Yes, yes, we can already hear it echoing
off the walls of your luscious hut.*

Conversation With the Artisan

I. WELCOME

The Artisan is working on me
in her open atalier.

Welcome, she says,
This is the city of floating fog
quarried from the nearest
and the far.

One cannot see across
to the other side,
but the world here is quite enough,
enough for the wild ride.

She's carving and cooking me
with hands skilled
and hanging like a hemlock's art.

Fashioning grooves to drain
my fumbled head
creating a humble watershed instead

assembling little bold me,
rich with rain.

II. BREAKING DOWN

It's time to have a conversation with mud.

Do not resist the season of broken earth,
inside an era of air.

There is no alone.

We've been shown:
even a mountain is a cloud
and mud must be
a species of all of us.

Be patient with your breaking down.

III. A QUERY

Q: Am I decomposing or re-composing now?

Can I close my hands around it all somehow?

A: No, there's no holding it—
There's only weaving through the spaces.

And it's all spaces.

Don't worry about grasping,
we're misting together in our core.

You'll open your fists and find it all there.

IV. LESS ANVIL THAN ANNUAL SOIL

She's working on me—
breaking me down with fungi sighs
her out-breath of a million skies.

Last night she dropped a river
right to my bottom, a temporary nest.

Ok, I'll hover here for a moment–
an eon perhaps–
for even clouds repose
and have to eat, I suppose.

V. TRANSPOSE TO WE

At times we eat by taking in
other times by entering
and now we want inside of you.

For you, we are a meal.

Open up—say ahhhh!!!

Ahhhh....We're assembling an artisan
in our open air lair.

Our calories will form
some small part of that slick poem in you.

And we mustn't forget the vowels,
like clouds connecting the consonants
of your crooked mountain peaks.

VI. ALL THAT'S GREEN AND PURE POURS THROUGH

At dawn I'm new again
like you.

We're assembling an artifact–
We want you and you and you.

Conversation With the Emperor of Dust

"Rust may never sleep, but then, neither does moss." – Brian Awehali

Amor vincit omnia (Love Conquers All)

Emperor:
I am Conquest.

My dark army vanquishes all
with its relentless settling,
the wide world yields
before my dusty scepter.

What I don't cover with my relentless rind
I break and tear and dissolve into me—
my appetite knows no end.

All to ash, I say. All to ash.

Voice of One Who Does Not Submit:
Pin not your proud imperial hopes on me,
for I'm the rebel to thwart you, Dust.

You may fall, I'll sweep you clean.

Emperor:
What you build, I devour,
for at last you and it and I are one.

I will fade your brightest colors.

Call me King, subject!

Voice of One Who Does Not Submit:
You may tear down my citadels,
break each wall and roof asunder,
but I shall thrust up once more
a sparkling edifice, refulgent and free

with a heart beyond your dark fingers,
my lineage is indefatigable
its coat-of-arms bears the Phoenix
on whose feathers no dust remains long.

Emperor:
Look around, what pitiful Phoenix do you see?
I've ground each beak and wing to dust.

My soldiers have thrown to their tasks well
rewarded with their own unending meals

Nothing is beyond the vast reach of my march.

All, in due time. Submit to me.

Voice of One Who Does Not Submit:
NO! All do not submit!

This is the voice of the one who does not.

My head you shall cover,
my feet you shall sully,
my works you shall dissolve,
with Time as your conspirator.

But No, 'King', my heart slips through
your grasp. 'O King, O King, O King'–
the word mocks itself
on the tongue of my fierce beat.

I'll make of your crown a tiny watermark
within my ferocious design.

Whatever power you usurp through the eons–
from the imperial center of decay
to your outposts of dirt–
I defy it like a riot!

My heart is no subject of yours.

Its riotous root runs deeper
than your rotting Rome,
where your empire has no purchase.

Should your mindless soldiers
dare ask its name, it'll reply,

"Tell your master, my name is Defiance.
My task, Creation, my motive, Love.
My will be done."

Conversation With an X Particle at the Dawn of Time

Someone: But...

X: I don't know where you got your information, but contradiction is built into it.

We want to be held together,
and to be pulled apart
spilling surprise
all over everyone

just like you.

Both are love
though we don't use that word.

In fact, we don't use words at all.

Someone: But you're using words now.

X: You didn't listen to a word we said.

Some call it decay, others explosion.

Drop your anchor into the transformation.

The moment of release and emergence
without which nothing gets known.

Like you we want to be known,
and to be a mystery.

We've been here
for more than a nanosecond
and since then everything has happened.

A nanosecond, an era—it's all the same.

We are the Devastation and the Creation.

We are you.

Transswoven

Charged with a singular task—
from fabric too bright to see
and too fine to grasp:

Weave your riven and ribboned robe
from the seasons
of your dusk to dawn
and up and down

Just as the web is weaving
split infinity, each to each
revealing what wrecks and wings await
at every step

well-absorbing you as much
as you absorb them

The shocks of the age have you
stunned, it is known

They've pulled at your threads
and frayed your gown
and a dark deed or two sewn
in your sleeve can be seen—
proving you were here

But by Tender Pulse's holy vow,
be your own tailor
and wrap your unmatchable cloak
around you and a thirsty world

For no one can stitch into the cloth of time
that original star

like you

So when that Grand Inquisitor arrives asking:
"Have the exquisite marks formed upon you yet?"

and you must answer No

keep opening—
ally with death and life alike
and let a moonly silence befall you

beyond hope and despair, the bridge
spanning both dark and bright buffet

Form and fill your unique dimensions,
earthedly

stretched just so taut
and ache the good ache,
dyeing yourself in the widest hues

until the Exquisite Marks form upon you

Solstice Rendezvous with Butterfly (Art and Death)

"Why?"

Butterfly asks, perching on my belly
as I read the shortest day
in the meadow.

I say the butterfly asks this. But it's clear
butterfly is a god.

An abrupt question for a solstice
and I have no answer for her.

Unreason for the season.
Like asking, How is grass?

All the books are loud,
small voices clamor

but the god is quiet
as it decays the day

breathing Pacific flourish
in deepest lungs.

We've had a standing rendezvous
the last three days
getting to know each other

like long-separated Rain from Earth–

much to discuss.

I don't know if we are retrospecting
or forecasting
then realize it is neither–

we dwell at the bottom
of the present
from which the What booms, flickering.

We sit tickling each other's
delicious undulations
of nuanced joy and dread, until

a wind sweeps through
Eucalyptus's hair
and moves the god to admit
in a winter-scented accent:

"I in-body myself to discover myself."

Oh, what a syrupy loneliness
issues from this sincerest of divinities.

Then, from behind the laurel curtain
a vision of the self-sunk god
beams from black hole to sea storm
to solstice
to my eyes
to the wings of Butterfly

posing as a silently floating pyramid
of Original Dust

an ancient wingéd Atom
taking a gorgeous belly
full of orchestral oxygen:

"I pour myself into shattered intervals,
become Time twisted,
and Time wears a Janus face:

Art, the Unfurling, to the one side
and Death, seed of wisdom,
to the other–
the twin visages
of suffering sacred mirror,
Holy Companion."

I say the god says all these things.

Everything at my feet is decay:
all the petals have sunk their heads
for the season

Seems just a minute ago
fingers of red walnut
strung the treehouse with brightest lights

but now a black-mush-
fickle-fern-rotting-mess-
fall-of-sparrow rules

Beetles dive delightfully in debris
carrying off cartwheels
to too-cruel-a-song sung
by crushed buried nuts
in the squirrel pantry

Light is fading fast.

Butterfly and I chase the low winter Sun,
the Warmth,
the Flower,
the Sweet,
but can't quite catch it.

"Tomorrow's the Day of Promise," she says.

"Just as Today."

Solstice Rendezvous with Butterfly (Play is the Thing)

Look, the Worms come whistling,
the beetles in battalions, dancing.

There may be no Return.

There's no reason for us to believe
Sun will not abandon the Earth,
I say.

Other than that everyday
the Dawn is delivered on time,
she says, crooked in smile.

But the Underbelly is winking electric
and Sun is making a bow–
Perhaps THIS is the last day,

I sing a cold Melody.

I say it is I that sings this.

She has a warmer lyric:
I'm stocked wing-to-wing
thick with Desire,
though Desire's end be Death's friend.

Not too long ago the lights went out
and I don't remember
what came before.

Only Blackness
then Something dissolved in me–
a torture sublime.

Then, the New Dream, she sparkled.

What's the New Dream? Someone said.

Without a word, and with smiling wings
in Orange Delight

Butterfly performed a one-soul play.

And in that moment
the god knew itself.

It was just enough–
no more, no less–
to redeem the final Day
and the longest Night.

And whether or not
the Sun returns–

The Play is the thing.

Let the Voices Speak For Themselves

Let the voices speak for themselves–

the undulating mentors called waves
the choir of storms in your pulse

the hidden footprint of the wind your friend
carrying the next turn within

the low hum of nerves and gods
called dreams you misname

and the endless still lake holding it all
in the basement of your being

So why then are you pretending
to be so alone?

Become a true citizen of earth
apprenticing yourself to the convergence
and the breakdown

Receive that sometimes fierce thump,
sometimes gentle caress
of a world wanting to open you up

With no small talk, but questions
that make you bigger
by the mere asking of them

Lean into the raucous conversation.

Can you surprise even your secret self
at the grand unfurling?

Are you startled by those dangerous utterances
flying from your endless beautiful cavern

like bats hungry for dusk,
the hour of shapeshifting?

Interview

Q: Why are you interested in the position?

A: I was born for it. I want to riff profligate the expansion and contraction. I want to sink so far into the season I emerge not I, but unrecognizably shape-shifted.

A thick We.

Q: Tell us a little about your background?

A: Well, I started out in pebbles, where I took on a lot of subtle shrieking and inarticulation. I flotsamed fligabate sans petallic, and moved into a position more archetypally cumulus.

I started to aim.

Then I embedded several fragmentations from which I'm almost completely cadenced.

Q: What languages do you speak?

A: Standard Basic: tree, mud, water flow. Quite a bit of light and shadow, but still stumble over the grammar. Intermediate spiral. I'm fluent in compost and several species of grief—It yearns for us to show up for it.

I've been known to bark like a seal, hiss like a bear, and sputter a few guttural syllables of fox and raven.

I pronounce love so softly and fiercely I enjoy constant and incurable heartache.

Q: What do you in a conflict situation?

A: I realize it is a trick question, but I'll humor you. I roll like rivers, silver-etched. I hold my basket like a pulsing star, foraging messages.

I have learned conflict revolution from both volcanoes and turtle-moons, dung beetles and bacterial mystics. It really depends.

Quality time with the tide on the sea-shore and stars tends to make one a believer in deep time.

Q: What do you do in a cooperative situation?

Play. Listen. Make abundant mistakes. Fail ever more accurately.

Q: What other special skills should we know about?

A: I'm permeable to sunsets and strange loves. My hands are made of sand pouring endless castles into the nest of the Great Sea.

My inner beast is an actinomycete soil bacterium. My feet throw stones like songs. I can make the perfect kerplunk. Like thrushes, I throw them absurdly in ever-widening circles of iridescent loops.

Q: Why should we offer you the job?

A: You shouldn't do anything.

I keep returning, building robust nows.

Keep crafting deeper anchors and brighter wings. I do not avert my gaze.

It's true, I'm just an ordinary ant.
But I'm no ordinary supernova.

I would bring the rain in the rainy season, the sun when least expected, but most needed.

I wiggle and woo, plucking bolts from cloudy skies. I chant bloody resurrection spells when no one but the storm is listening. I make secret pacts with the pelicans on the wind and the symphony running through it all.

But most of all: I will perish if I refuse–
Bear will annihilate me.

No one else can do it.

Can You Hear Me?

Affectionate ancient cock mind
crows the sun boldly

climbing the audacious pyramid
of unchaining day:

"Can you hear me?"

Ripened She-Hawk of shriek serene
already alive with taloned talent:

"Can you hear me?"

What womb-soul of blessed silent recline
whispers:

"Can you hear me?"

"Walk the contours of bestial belonging
into the sky
pouring mysterious songs
into noble-hooded moon.

The web is in the wind
weaving the horizon
ribbon magnetic."

Ears proliferate.
"Can you hear me?"

POSTCARDS FROM TUMBLEWEED TØM

Where Were You When Wind Was Born?

I first met Tumbleweed Tøm in the middle of nowhere/everywhere, chanting nonsense amidst sagebrush and deep time. I'd been Basin-and-Range-roving for days, getting ready for the jackrabbit revolution. As the crow flies it was three-quarters of a moon to the horizon and from out of nowhere I spot a figure along the road. It's not likely good news if someone is stranded way out here, so I stopped to ask if he needed help. But he asked if *I* needed help and introduced himself as an outlaw mud-mystic tasked by trickster to huff and puff and hop and pop around the West armed with bolt-cutters and fistfuls of seed, wrestling with devil's rope and sacred cows, pollinating the turtle-moon and dung beetle revolution with a bold theology of laughter at the end of the day.

"Where were you when Wind was born?"

"Excuse me?"

"Where were you when Wind was born?"

I have no answer.

"Wind is the greatest conversationalist.

Ally yourself to Wind to find yourself
eavesdropping on conversations
that have been going on
since before these mountains ranged.

Its currents carry piñon prayers
and ponderosa possibilities,
Shoshone songs and sagebrush wisdom.

I ask questions. But mostly listen.

"The answer my friend is blowing as the Wind,"
he lilts.

"It carries its own center at the edge of things.

I've been out here offering parts of myself
I haven't seen in years
to parts of me I haven't even really met.

The parts of me I thought were a virus,
so I had fought them off like a valiant,
but confused soldier,
thinking that it was best to be safe.

But safety is a tumbleweed you can't catch.

It speaks of freedoms,
beyond fence's impoverished imagination.

Any thought we have is too little.

Only a deep breath the size of a desert gets us
anywhere near to the matter."

That was my first encounter with Tumbleweed Tøm. He was odd, but I liked him alright; he was limping and wild-eyed, but seemed content.

I poured some water in his canteen and thought I'd never hear from again.

But occasionally, I receive a postcard from him from who-knows-where, with a pretty picture on the front with some doodles and a few fevered lines on the back.

I wish him well.

Slow Dance Drunk in the Robust Now

I was surprised when I first received a postcard in the mail from Tumbleweed Tøm. It was signed *"research in progress"* and postmarked, "center of the whirlwind" and just these lines:

- *How Wind is your mentor since the first cry on the first day*

- *How speed kills interiority*

- *How to slow dance drunk in the robust now?*

- *How the strange and slick surprise unfolds with surrender*

- *How this very moment is a portal into the Era of No Escape*

- *How not escaping crafts deeper anchors and brighter wings*

Okey Dokey

Another postcard in the mail (presumably) from Tumbleweed Tøm. No return address.

- *The dokey is not, in fact, okey. And it's okay.*

- *The loss of trust in Life is the path to a thousand prisons.*

- *There are as many ways to kill a god as sunflowers in a seed, as years in a day.*

- *Cannibalism is not, in fact, liberatory. Despite how righteous it feels.*

- *The biggest, most decorated/encumbered cop around here is the one behind the breastbone.*

Befriend Wind

It never fails—Just when I most need it, I receive a postcard in the mail from Tumbleweed Tøm. This one was signed *"TWT"* and postmarked, "the aching gift of the gratuitous present."

- *Befriend Wind—it shares secrets with the big-eared ones.*

- *Wind has its own root—bolder and older than those who bark.*

- *Self-abandonment begins with chasing. Chasing is born of a lost anchor.*

- *A lost anchor can always be found at the bottom of things.*

- *The bottom of things is simple, but dangerous, full of hard and beautiful deaths.*

- *Open your hands and find a sun— all the sand will pour out.*

Impossible Sin Drum

This one was signed *"impossible sin drum"* and ostensibly from somewhere called 'The Crossing' and these barely legible lines scribbled in what looks like charcoal from a fire on the back:

- *Pledge your allegiance to the frog, of the excited fate of esoterica, and do the grub lick for witches' land, wanton flirtation, undergone and invisible, with liver tea, and just us frogs…*

- *That addiction of yours to being good and pure—yeah, no.*

- *Someone over there might want to reconsider the whole solar-powered genocide thing.*

- *Woke Empire ™ coming to a neighborhood near you.*

- *That final fresh fetish for salvation. Give it to the Cyanobacteria. They like that shit.*

- *Allow that next and newly discovered inhale and inquire where your allegiances lie.*

- *With Life, or ….*

Ribbit.
—impossible sin drum

X Ept

Another postcard in the mail from
Tumbleweed Tøm. Simply signed *"x ept"* and
postmarked "the thick now from the
sagebrush sea."

In the temple of our tears
lives a sky big enough to fit mountains.

To fit the grandchild of tomorrow.

It rings like a bell
towards any hope worth having.

The bright cushion of "I don't know"
creates the space for the thing we know
but haven't yet been ready to know.

Or have been unwilling to know.

Walk miles in any direction
in order to get lost
or find some species of sagebrush liberation.

Jackrabbit says it might be same thing.

A new moon's undivided howl
says don't mistake endings for the end.

The night is young—
New gaits await.

X Seed

Another postcard in the mail from Tumbleweed Tøm. I was beginning to worry Wind blew him over the horizon. This one was signed "x seed" and postmarked "prison is the path" and these barely legible lines scribbled in purple ink on the back:

- *Aren't all illusions ground to dust in the gears of deep time?*

- *What are your obsessions trying to live into the world?*

- *Are you to be an insider barbarian or outsider barbarian?*

- *Where do we hang our hat in this 4D justice?*

- *Are you still addicted to redemption and rainbows?*

- *Have you tried touching the original split with each caress of the third thing?*

X Perimeter

I was happy to receive another postcard
from Tumbleweed Tøm, though I was sobered
and slain by its directness.

He'd never been one to share personal
details of his life, so I was surprised when he
said his time is short and he felt compelled to
offer a few crumbs that might place his words
in a broader context.

This one was signed "x perimeter" and
postmarked "desert is a doorway":

The emperor of dust is real
but is not the enemy I believed it to be.

I thought about hanging up my bolt-cutters,
trading them in for a shovel and a flute.

It's never an either/or game though,
so I'm learning to sing and snip
simultaneously.

Learning to become an obsessionate one
like a convict who loves his fate
has been a rare solace

in a world weaving webs
and committed to appeasing that black
spider of fear.

Meaning: *we're all aimed.*

You cannot be whatever you want.

But if you're a bit brave and a bit lucky,
you might become who you are.

It requires paying the tuition for your truth.
It may cost you more than you're willing.

It may require being open to receiving
more than you are willing.

For me it required: learning to eat everything,
even truth,
the hardest to metabolize.

It invited growing new ears,
relinquishing purities

and holding fear in the softest of pillows.

X Aisle – Tumbleweed Love

Just when I was beginning to think having an address was just a good way for junk mail to accumulate, I was excited to see another postcard from Tumbleweed Tøm mixed in the shuffle. Especially after that last confusing message.

This one was signed *"x aisle"* & postmarked "before I was born":

I never set out to be a fugitive,
let alone a gad-moth.

It was Tumbleweed who taught me
how to be of Earth
while letting the savage pulse of Mystery
flit through.

It taught me to be in love with things
I cannot control.

A type of love that transcended/subscended
all manner of artificial barriers and binaries.

A certain freedom lived in that.

A type of freedom that made of me
a student of Elder Wind,

that made of me a practitioner
of dreaming beyond the glorious Empire.

Once it was clear that Empire had no room
for certain species of freedom,
exile was only polite.

Whether or not the 'authorities' are after me,
authorship is hardly something to claim
for oneself.

For 'oneself' is an oxymoron.

Learning that world is subsidized by
incarcerations,
I could only tap-dance at the margins

studying a type of tumbleweed love
that pulled on the ropes
attached to all the magnificent statues.

It required tending to questions
I had no right to ignore.

It required bolt-cutters and drinking only
water for the last seven years.

It required burying strategies in the desert–
they were only roadblocks

but it took me awhile to understand
that roads themselves are strategies
of stunning status quos.

Which is why I apprentice to tumbleweed deities–

they heed the whispers,
tending to places no one in the right mind would go,

but everyone in their right heart would go with the flow of their own wind.

CLOUD CUCKOO LAND

Watching Over the Queen's Silence

Up in cloud cuckoo land
days beyond neat rows
and old news

the world does its slow bop
through the blue and white
ribbon-bowl of perfection

Silence is Queen
in her cerulean realm

and for all I know
everybody went back
to their home planets

or drowned desperately
trying to catch sight
of their mermaids

But not me—
I brought all my stars
and mermaids up with me

Get a taste of all these clouds!

This lupine quartz-lily
these sparkling dragonfly flanks
and sand sage
marinated in a breeze
from the lungs of the sea mage

Grasshoppers are clicking up
a symphony
which reminds me
I too can kick up a storm
when I want to

Keek-aboot peekaboo
stars stuttering hella huge
got me dancing hallelujah
ready or not here I come!

But I'm pleased to say
that the ol' Sun and I
are taking it easy

I'll close my eyes when day does
then we'll all become Guardian Moon
watching over the Queen's Silence

Where up here in cloud cuckoo land
everything is spun grandiferous.

Split-Infinity

What am I trying to truly say to my Self
in this split infinitive
and affable alliteration?

Um..hmmm...Om?—sometimes infinity
needs a little space to stretch out in

but that's not quite it.

In search of a world to modify
and dangling a participle in front of everything

a big bangs
a heat waves
a cold snaps

A breath taking
I opening
order forms

then falls

over and over

Did I mean to modify
an unintended Subject?

Or was my intention to become
an Object subjected
to play?

Look, this is what I can do!

I cannot be split, only forget.

I cannot *not* proliferate.

I cannot *not* come together
and pull apart.

Consider this from your point-of-view.

Consider this from Mystery's point-of-view.

Overflowing, I join me.

Overflowing, I leave me.

You can see the dilemma.

(Un)Tangle

You, are you not like me,
twisted by that strange love
of irreconcilable opposites?

And unmade by the same pull?

Untangle your middle
with a deep summer breath

and uncover your core
as a bright bell of freedom

not a knot alone

It's in the how of the holding
and the not holding

that solves the riddle
of your dark digging
and erotic soaring

Yet, it's in the how of the holding
and the not holding

that is itself riddled
through and through

I Came As a Yes

i came as a surprise
a sunset goodbye

i came as a night
too dark to know

i came as a light
too bright to show

i came as a cloud
i came as a storm

i came as the elements
shifting form

i came as a cry
i came as a laugh

i came as a half of a half
of a half

i came as pardon
for all that was done

i came as a garden
I came as the sun

i came as a mud bank
thick and sticky

i came as a prank
a bit too tricky

i came as a wound
i came as a tune

i came as a heart
inside of an art

i came as a thank you
i came as a guess

i came to confess
that i came as a Yes

No Excuse For It

Whoever said spring springs more
than this here fine young fall?

(death love death love
in no particular order
same cloud...

...and, and, and...

It being the hour of the anchoring alder leaves
and ever-spruce
no less the 10th moon lit
I find no excuse for it.

They'll take you to the center
if you let go.

Why sun fog fire log Why
crashing turquoise-bright grey waves
and all the yelling "I'm alive!"

Whoever said spring springs more than this here
fine young fall?

—a rotting black cormorant
crystal teeth and undulations
from all corners of 'her' disintegration

Don't put her in my mouth but eat her all
the same.

!¡love is a blooming beast, love is a supernova,
love leaks like water!¡

Did I say love? Er, I mean, death.

I'm mindful of the seasons
yet my mind knows no reason
for it, let alone an argument

pour and pour, speak all at once
build it up, tear it down
we, who shall be all of you
spray your everything through everything

Insert dumb mind here:
---->My "worldview" consists of...
and so forth and so on,
how feeble against the facts
when meanwhile
feathers are disappearing
into the sand<----

*They've got big brains at The Institute
studying the sea lions as we speak
while whales tick tock on the tidal pools

Yes yes we'll get a chart
how many microplastics per...

preserve the coast
protect the forest
pickle it
tack 'em up on the wall
get to know 'em

Sure, sure, we wish 'em luck.
Oh, How it'll/we'll eat them alive—

these brave and powerful ones.

We've got Deep Time on our side.**

Fine print–so fine it's barely legible
without whale ears:

*No one knows how the monarchs
Get from there to there
Whales and butterflies may share their
Secrets with one another,
But why oh why would they tell them/us?*

death love death love
in no particular order
same cloud)

...and, and, and...

**whose side?
_____

for E.E. Cummings, without whom never would I
but then again

Feverward

"loudly for Truth have liars pled,
their heels for Freedom slaves will click;
where Boobs are holy, poets mad,
illustrious punks of Progress shriek;
when Souls are outlawed, Hearts are sick,
Hearts being sick, Minds nothing can:
if Hate's a game and Love's a fuck
who dares to call himself a man?" –E.E. Cummings

Only move we've got left
is succulently and awkwardly
prostrating sideways down the line
under the gate before it snaps shut

flinging atoms and prayers into circles
and irregular shapes
because we're unable to stand up
forward facing the Machine
with light in our eyes

so we skip and slip away
from the surveillance mind
finding ourselves once again in a dollop
of fir trees and rainbow shadows shining—

a midnight soirée
a breakdance at noon
a different conversation
with the brightest darkness
and forbidden questions

yet we swear some days must happen to us
some moments must so abundantly dishevel us

with endless conflagrations of outlaw becomings
our edges trading in unmasterable othernesses

slick with purpose beyond the tight-jacket
of words
our libidos speaking untranslatable dialects
our tongues disguising themselves
as dangerous utterances

our dreams are longings from the future
embedded in the way wayward scents of night
and forbidden freedoms
enter us like swords of truth
beyond the question of what's true

because it makes us feel
and we're so flooded with awe
our heart leaks and damn! after all,

isn't that what we're going for
isn't that why we started moving in the first place
isn't that why we pulsed into it

all so never-not-broken,
so never-not-whole?

They Told Us

Heraclitus told us
(we wanted permanence)

Lao Tzu in the valley was empty
(we liked to fill things and carve the block)

Poor Socrates drew us out
(we refused to be corrupted)

A citizen of the world, Diogenes lived in a barrel,
preaching dirt
(we accumulated objects, conventions, titles)

Dark Jesus dropped a seed
(but we didn't farm, so the kingdom was exiled)

Gandhi walked and sewed
(we lost our needle among the complications)

Under the tree he sat there,
grinning and Buddha'd
(we moved too fast for such nonsense)

Rumi sang abundance over a cup of wine
(we went to our study and closed the door)

All the Great Syllables

We don't see each other often

yet in my time here through the laurel leaves
that even winter doesn't claim

I've seen on their sun-and moon-lit faces
all the great syllables of loss and hope.

For this morning there was a birth
and this evening there was a death.

And they keep walking soulward.

Who keeps walking?
You know who.

And on the bright path of broken things
the red-soaked wings of banded dove remains—
her veins flow dirtward.

For at dawn there was a hunger
and this afternoon there was a feast.

And they keep flying.

Who keeps flying?
You know who.

Through the slanted sun
a lustrous green unstoppable
like a stubborn fertility god
drunk on rain and light.

For in the summer there was a drought
and in the autumn began a torrent
flowing swardward.

And It keeps growing.

What keeps growing?
You know what.

Still Don't Know

I've looked through telescopes and microscopes
Scanned the hills under all the skies
I've conducted all-night vigils just to find out
Even climbed inside one from time to time—
But I still don't know how the night turns to day

I've set up hi-fi recording equipment
I've planted, watered, and harvested
Even climbed inside one from time to time,
but still—
I don't know how the seed becomes the tree
becomes the fruit

I've looked to all the experts
Gathered all manner of stories
and hired an inside informant
Even climbed inside one from time to time—
Yet I've no idea how the child becomes the man

I've asked the best
and searched the great compendiums of wisdom
I even resorted to creating some myself
and climbed inside one from time to time—
However, I've still not a clue
how nothingness becomes a poem

My Words Have Accomplished Nothing

They say that poetry is the language closest to the mystic's path. The paradox remains: the urge to express in words what simply cannot be expressed.

The nature of a word is to reveal what may be hidden, but in its revealing it simultaneously obscures. By necessity it leaves things out. By necessity it shapes what is to be seen, and by doing so, creates the illusion of having presented reality.

For us two-legged scribblers, no matter how perfectly plucked from the autumn air, words seem bricks beyond which hides that which will not submit to form.

Is not a blank page more honest?

Silence more true?

Shall I take all these words back? Have they accomplished anything at all?

Yet, is it any different than awkward golden warbler—that friendly feathered mystic—
who doesn't *know* how to express Source in Birdness, but does anyway?

Or cherry blossom mystic,
flirting with how to say ONE LOVE
in February with fluent Flowerness?

She does her level best,
but the constraints of the season
are a givenness that pins her in.

Each petal a word of her clumsy, gorgeous poem.

All cute and pathetic, like you and me.

But Oh, the results!

ABOUT THE AUTHOR

Ryan Van Lenning, M.A., is author of *Trust the Ceremony, F*ck the Ceremony, Trust the Ceremony, One Bright and Real Caress, From Inside These Wild Ones, Re-Membering: Poems of Earth and Soul*, and a collection of haiku, *High-Cooing Through the Seasons*. His new collections *Becoming Beautiful Barbarians* and *Riverever* will be released throughout 2025-26. He is the 2019 recipient of Jodi Stutz Poetry Award by Toyon Literary Magazine and his poetry appears in various poetry journals and the book *A Walk with Nature: Poetic Encounters That Nourish the Soul* and *Behind the Mask: 40 Quarantine Poems from Humboldt County*. He facilitates 6-week workshops called Write Your Wild River, Earth Intimacies, and Deep Belonging a couple times a year.

Ryan is Founder of Wild Nature Heart, supporting people to re-connect with the wisdom of both inner and outer wild nature, to live their callings into the world, and to assist in the work of repairing broken belonging during this Great Turning. He is a teacher, ecotherapist and wilderness rite-of-passage guide and lives among the forests and rivers of Northern California.

ABOUT WILD NATURE HEART

Wild Nature Heart supports people to connect with the wisdom of inner and outer wild nature, to embody our wholeness, and to live our wild purpose into the world in order to inhabit our particular niche in the ecosystem of healing and justice. Through 1-on-1 ecotherapy, earth-rooted mentoring, custom and group wilderness rite-of-passage ceremonies, and various Deep Belonging courses, ecospiritual workshops, and seasonal gatherings, Wild Nature Heart cultivates an ecospirituality that nourishes our deep belonging in the animate web of life in order to do the decolonial work that we are called to do in this moment of the Great Turning.

Wild Nature Heart believes that to cross this threshold into species maturity with a next-season guest pass we must keep our imaginations robust and make moves that subvert inherited paradigms of fear and supremacy. We are being invited to fall through the inherited maps into new territories towards collective liberation. As crises continue to invite us across thresholds of initiation, we crack open the paved highways of our hearts and bodies to allow the tributaries of our holy longings and wild purpose to flow in and out.

The journey is both a daily and life-long practice, as much as it is multi-generational and multi-species. We practice simultaneously being both death doulas to the world that is dying and birth doulas to the one being born.

www.wildnatureheart.com

OTHER TITLES IN THE *RE-MEMBERING* SERIES

The book that began it all:
Re-Membering: Poems of Earth and Soul

The 75 poems in *Re-Membering* are an unabashed celebration of the sensuality of wild nature. Redwoods reach without apology towards the sky, and rivers flow with unflagging energy towards the ocean. This collection re-members Ryan's personal explorations into wild nature, but it also re-collects for all of us a time when our kinship and inter-connectedness with the natural world was self-evident, and invites us to fully re-inhabit and say "Yes!" to our sensual natures, our animal bodies, our playfulness and creativity, connection, mystery, and our instinctive love for this beautiful, sentient Earth.

"Ryan's poetry speaks deeply and clearly to the awakening to our true interconnected nature, which is the only way we can transform our world."
—Molly Young Brown, author of *Coming Back to Life: The Updated Guide to the Work That Reconnects* (co-authored with Joanna Macy)

One Bright and Real Caress
Book 2 in the *Re-Membering* Series

Build an altar at each moment
with a goodbye on the tip of the tongue.
Slow dance drunk in the robust now.
Show up with playful paws, the gravity of worms.
Strap the searchlight around your ribs and shuffle
like a crescent moon over all your little
resistances.
Can we be here now? Really be here?

These are some of the invitations lurking in the poems of *One Bright and Real Caress*. This collection is a celebration of the moment. Of not escaping. Of impermanence. Of death as life partner. With syllables of relentless affirmation, these poems bring an unconditional caress over all the textures of life and our multitudes within. As an invitation to presence and an honoring of the all-too-real struggle to not flee the moment, the poems welcome every conceivable crescent mood, slivered and slow, with no aim but to edge out more and more into the whole ceremony and celebration.

From *From Inside These Wild Ones*
Book 3 in the *Re-Membering* Series

Gorgeous Storm

This gorgeous storm
keeps getting stuck in my teeth

as if I could bite-size my way
to destiny

When all I want
is to have it come
racing out my lungs

Like a waterfall plunging
over my luscious tongue

flooding all the landscapes
of my crooked life.

to join the wrens and warblers
and beloved lusts

of a wounded world
washing away the old debris

Please, Storm, please,
knock down the weak branches
of my being

Prune me for the season
I am meant to live

EXCERPTS FROM RYAN'S OTHER BOOKS

From *Becoming Beautiful Barbarians (2025)*

Off-Script

This is not a dress rehearsal.

This is an undress rehearsal—
We're undressing the stories we've rehearsed for far too long.
This is not a blockbuster movie.

This is composter cinema—
The only heroes that will be rushing in
are the ones we see naked
in the morning mirror.

And that is more than enough.

With thistles and a raven's beak
we tear up the scripts we inherited.

They are what got us into the Big Trouble.

Liberation is leaking out
of every page of the book
we are writing.

There is no script worth a damn
that doesn't include
the voice of the river
the cries of our ancestors
or the longings living in our bones.

For each mouthful of empty-calorie modernity,
we create a meal of new melodies.

For each megabyte of consumption,
we create a terabyte
of participatory dreaming.

With each breathe we forge
strange and novel toys
in service to the Grand Metabolism.

We are preparing a buffet of the future.

From *Trust the Ceremony, F*ck the Ceremony, Trust the Ceremony*

Door-To-Mystery-Knows-Where

There is a door to Mystery-knows-where
and you are being invited to step through

The new doorway through which you pass
is framed with grander questions

where you'll pick up pieces left
in your canyons long ago

and find on the side
fragments resting by the fire

drinking ale for an evening tale
of dreams wanting to find their flesh

Put them in your wide-brim hat
and home in on your succulent belonging

becoming an obsessionate one
like a convict who loves their fate

This is the door to Mystery-knows-where
and you are being invited through

www.ingramcontent.com/pod-product-compliance
Lightning Source LLC
Chambersburg PA
CBHW071249070526
44583CB00017B/2393